Networking

EXPRESS

Networking Express

Networking

EXPRESS

Know How to Network with People for
Business, Career, and Success

Laura Stafford & KnowIt Express

N2K Publication

ISBN 978-1-534-73863-8

Printed in the United States of America

First Edition

Welcome to the *Know It Express* - the express lane to knowledge!

To stay up-to-date, please be sure to sign up for **our newsletter** at http://www.KnowItExpress.com and follow us on social media:

https://www.facebook.com/KnowItExpress
https://twitter.com/KnowItExpress
https://plus.google.com/+KnowItExpress

EXPRESS LANE

CHAPTER 1 - Starting a Network

11 - Before The Social Network

12 - Self-Evaluation: Know Your Network

CHAPTER 2 - The Making of a Network

15 - Structure Of Networking

17 - Exercise: Create Your Professional Map

19 - Taking The Next Steps

CHAPTER 3 - Objective and Tools

21 - Your Mojos

23 - Create Your Elevator Sales Pitch

27 - Tools Of The Trade

CHAPTER 4 - Online Networking

30 - Extend Your Limitless Reach Virtually

32 - Closing-The-Loop In Online Networking

CHAPTER 5 - Offline Networking

35 - Out In The Jungle

37 - Working The Room

40 - It's A Networker's World

CHAPTER 6 - Follow-Up and Repeat

44 - Maintenance

46 - Polylogue

CHAPTER 7 - Closing a Network

49 - David And Goliath

50 - A Networker's Checklist

Networking Express

Networking Express

CHAPTER 1

Starting a Network

Before The Social Network

Professional arena or market space is dynamic and virtual - people are changing, roles are shifting, processes are evolving, rules of the game are fluctuating and so you need to constantly keep pace with the world around you.

Yet the hype has been here for years! All this noise about **networking** is not misplaced.

Networking is key in building professional success and has been long before social media or the Internet came into existence. (Alumni groups and good ol' boys clubs have given way to LinkedIn and professional networks.)

From businessmen to politicians, from students to freelancers, from headhunters to job seekers, everyone is doing some kind of networking.

Question is…are YOU? Or rather - are you doing any productive or effective networking?

Let's find out!

<u>Self-Evaluation</u>: Know Your Network

1.) Except for being a hermit, you'll need to network to achieve your goals. So what is your immediate professional goal that requires networking? Is it an internship, increased sales or getting nominated for something? Perhaps you want to be an educator…a financial planner…a singer?

2.) Excluding your friends, who are five professional contacts that will *give you* that critical 'extra' support for your professional goals? This may include professional recommendations, customer referrals, introductions to industry leaders, or even just calling in a favor.

3.) What are the professional goals of other people in your network?

4.) Now, keep thinking of more professional contacts and continue adding to each list. After you've run out of names, compare the two lists – which one has more people?

Hold on to this <u>exercise and the list</u>, we will come back to it later.

If you're reading this, chances are that you're intimidated by the formidable task at hand…or you don't even know where to start.

Stop worrying!

Starting **now** and meeting a few professional contacts will help you gain some quality ground TODAY. So let's break it down step by step.

CHAPTER 2

The Making of a Network

Structure Of Networking

In the most basic of definitions, networking is a system of connecting people. But let's look a little more in-depth.

1. **The Purpose of Networking.** <u>Professional improvement, growth or change</u>. No matter who you are in the professional world, you're working towards one of these goals. From getting a promotion to finding a new job, from increasing your customer base to engaging investors, from getting elected to an office to lobbying for a cause...networking is ubiquitous.

2. **Nature of a Network.** <u>Connections</u>. Without even consciously thinking about it, everyone plays a multitude of roles – customer, user, patron, guide, and so much more. The unique thing about networking is that it does not have a hierarchy – it's the equalizer.

3. **Networking Input.** <u>Quality and quantity</u>. Building a productive network takes time, persistence, and sometimes money. That's why planning, prioritizing and executing are *so very* critical.

4. **Results.** <u>Measurable and tangible</u>. Since networking is done with a purpose behind it *(your objectives and career goals)*, you're working towards some very real results. Look at how many people are in your network and then look at how many are in those people's networks. The chain is ever growing and you can reach out for your connections.

5. **Networking.** <u>Cyclical and multidirectional</u>. With changing objectives and goals, networking strategies

and audiences also shift. No matter how long you've been networking, you're always a first-timer when you're pursuing a new goal. While being part of your own network, you're also a node in someone else's network.

The Six Degrees of Separation Theory has never been more relevant than today. Because of the interconnectivity of the world, you're only six steps away from any person on the planet.
So it's safe to say that's it's not just what you know, it is also who you know.

Exercise: Create Your Professional Map

Alright, we're getting warmed up now. So, it's clear that any person engaged in networking is doing it to either *meet their goals* or to *accelerate their growth*. When there is already a purpose established, then it's a no-brainer to have a plan in place for it.

Here are a few components to your professional map:

1.) What are your 5-year professional goals?
- Write a list of your short-term and long-term objectives.
- Remember to add milestones for learning as well as achievements.

2.) What makes you stand out from the contemporary crowd?

3.) Create a "virtual reputation" that fits who you are.
- Any online representation of yourself.

4.) Who are the top 3-5 leaders you need to connect with, who can enable your goals?

This map will help keep you focused on your purpose and direction.

Taking The Next Steps

Now let's follow this person who we will call 'Jordan' on the networking trail as she pursues her first job after completing her Undergrad degree.

Having majored in business, Jordan is keen on sales and finance opportunities. During both her junior and senior year, she successfully interned at a B2B company and a cooperative bank.

Unfortunately, she does not have any job offers at the moment and is graduating in two months. She has created profiles on various social networks, such as: LinkedIn, Facebook, and Twitter.

Over the next 24 hours, Jordan will work on expanding her network.

There are four approaches she will use:

1.) Objectives and Tools

2.) Online Networking

3.) Offline Networking

4.) Follow-Up and Repeat

Let's get started…

CHAPTER 3

Objective and Tools

Your Mojos

There are many questions that should help Jordan on her networking journey and they may help you as well. Some of those are:

- How are you going to introduce yourself?
- Where should you start – send an email or meet face-to-face?
- What are the important things to say when you first *network* with someone?
- When is a good time to send your résumé?

- How many times can you follow up with the same person?

In both <u>your case</u> and in <u>Jordan's</u>, you need to make sure you have a clear understanding of your goals, your skills, what you can offer and what requests you're going to make. You should only need one or two hours to work through the following:

- Build clarity about your professional interests. For Jordan, that would be jobs in sales and finance.

- Next, review any open job opportunities in your city where you are qualified to apply – take notes about what are the important skills or job requirements.

- Prepare your résumé so that the points you are making align with what the jobs are asking for. Highlight areas where you are well suited for the job as per the requirements mentioned.

Create Your Elevator Sales Pitch

All of networking, its purpose and success, lives inside of language. In the message you design and the ideas you spread. There are 3 important components for an effective networking introduction:

1. Your Name and Skills.

Examples:

- "Hi, I'm Jordan Smith. I just completed my business management degree from Rice University. I majored in finance and really enjoy sales too."

- "Hi, I'm Ken from the League City chapter of the Red Cross. I manage the fund raising initiatives for our blood donations and commercial donations across west Houston. It's been a very successful year and we've seen an increase in corporate support this past year."

- "Hi, I'm Linda from Proactive Marketing. I founded this company after spending a dozen years consulting with fortune 100 companies for their new product launches."

2. Your Purpose.

Examples:
- "I'm looking for a role in B2B sales. I have previously interned with the Yellow Pages product division and exceeded all my customer service goals. I'd really like to know more about the career opportunities at your outside sales division."

- "My team has been at the forefront serving the Houston communities in the aftermath of the floods and we are stretched beyond our resources and reserves. It's my goal to engage with corporations and enable their donations to reach the communities in need."

- "I'm looking to partner with start-ups who are in need of marketing leadership for anchoring their products against large competitors in the market."

3. How You Can Contribute to the People You Network With.

Examples:

- "Some very successful leaders and staff in your organization are alumni of my school and can speak for the quality of our education. My academic record, including my two internships, is stellar. My previous employers are happy to send out strong recommendations regarding my performance. I'm excited to start my career in this industry."

- "I understand that a large part of your staff was affected by the floods and you are concerned about their safety. Partnering in rescue operations, with your finances and our expertise, will enable you to impact a larger community."

- "Being a new business myself, I understand that start-ups are high on passion and initiative, but need external expertise in a few areas. I can help them identify their product placement strategy to enable strong results at a budget investment meeting."

To create your message, first write down an introduction draft in your own words.

Read it to yourself out loud in front of a mirror to see how you come across because seeing it as plain text is one thing, but performing it live is another.

- You can also watch Shark Tank episodes to understand how entrepreneurs introduce and pitch their business in the first 60 seconds.

Identify your style, refine your message and create an introduction that feels both comfortable and effective.

Tools Of The Trade

Part of being a successful networker is knowing how the world works, which is becoming increasingly technological, so it's important to keep up with the times.

What do you need to network effectively in this internet age?

1. **A website.** You can hire someone to build you a page and you can buy a domain name. You can also easily find free sites such as:

about.me

tumblr.com

WordPress.com

TIP: about.me actually has an app that serves as a virtual business card.

2. **Social media.** Regardless of what you decide to do, having an online identity is extremely important. Along with having a website comes having social media. In a world where people are tweeting more than reading, you cannot have enough social media presence. The good news is, most social media platforms are free.

A.) **LinkedIn.** A must-have for every professional networker.

B.) **Twitter.** Twitter is great because people can "follow" you. You want followers, because in this world, followers = influence.

C.) **Facebook page.** You want to have a professional Facebook page, one that people can "like," separate from your personal Facebook profile.

D.) **Instagram (if applicable).** This app is for artists or businesses with a visual focus.

3. **Smartphone.** It will make your life a whole lot easier because many social media platforms and nifty apps go hand in hand with having a smartphone. Plus, it doesn't have to be state of the art and is more affordable than you think! Verizon and AT&T have plans where you can buy a smartphone and pay as you go. If it doesn't work out, you can always just use the smartphone simply as a MP3 player or organizer.

Now that you have these tools, it's time to dive into online networking.

CHAPTER 4

Online Networking

Extend Your Limitless Reach Virtually

The low-hanging fruit in networking are online platforms, such as LinkedIn. These can be very helpful, and they are specially equipped with several features to help job seekers or first time networkers.

Online networking only takes a few hours of your time, but it can really prep the playing field for you. When you enhance your online presence, it already gives you an edge because people associate it with real world results and interactions.

If you haven't been very proactive so far in online networking, then the following steps will benefit you in the long run:

- Use the information on your résumé to update or create your online professional profile. Make sure to clearly state that you are looking for job opportunities within a specific domain (ex. Sales). Make sure you post a professional picture of yourself within your online profile. Also, go through your personal social media accounts and remove anything that may be inappropriate or controversial. Recruiters <u>WILL</u> look at your social media pages, so make sure the material posted on them does not embarrass you.

- Connect with colleagues and leaders from previous companies where you either worked or interned. Ask them about any open opportunities that they have or that they know about where your skills will be a good fit.

- Positive recommendations from previous employers or school faculty will help you on your journey forward.

- Ask around and see if your closest contacts know of anyone else they can introduce you to who might be able to help you land a job in your desired field.

- Networking events and online professional groups will help you get in touch with and mingle with the contacts you want to make. These people are in your desired industry. Go talk to them!

Closing-The-Loop In Online Networking

While online networking has many benefits, there are a few drawbacks too. The length and quality of your message, other people's engagement with what you have to say, and the time it takes to network and follow up are all variable factors.

Two things that online networking does well: **endorsement** and **introduction**. There are many ways to network and find people who can endorse you.

Here are a few ways to accomplish that:

1. Cash In On Your Merit And Make A Request

- "Professor Chase, your recommendation about my research work and lab supervision will go a long way in helping me secure this internship."

- "Thank you for your business. I really enjoyed the assignment. Your testimonial at the conference or a customer referral would be much appreciated as I grow my clientele."

2. Return A Recommendation

- "After a whole week of training clients, I love to pamper my sore muscles with some spa time at Angelina's. I highly recommend them and conveniently, they're right across the street from our facility."

- "Many of our spa customers and staff are regulars at the Body Works CrossFit. They really give you a good workout.

Remember the <u>self-evaluation</u> you did at the beginning? Get it out now and decide whom on that list to request a recommendation or an introduction from.

CHAPTER 5

Offline Networking

Out In The Jungle

Offline networking is a very potent option for building long-term professional connections. It also takes the most time and effort. Meeting and talking with others who have similar professional goals is the most powerful kind of networking.

Sometimes it just involves being at the right place at the right time.

Focus in and strategize on who you want to contact and why. This rule is indispensible.

Now going back to Jordan...

Jordan is dressed in smart professional attire and attending an after-hours networking event for B2B sales folks at a local golf club. She sees a sea of faces. They all seem to be talking to each other or engaged with someone else. Many of these people are very experienced in their field.

How should she meet someone? What will she say? How long should she stick to one person or group before moving to the next? How many people should she meet during this two hour social? What can she say that will help her connect to her first job or next opportunity?

So how would you scan the room, select people to speak with, and prioritize your connections?

Working The Room

1. Enter the Networking Event and Head for the Registration Table. Generally, people at the registration desk are easy to talk to. Sometimes they even know the bigwigs who are attending. It is possible that the registration hosts are the organizers for the social gathering. The registration desk will not only sign you in, but they will get you set up with the schedule for the full event. On the off chance that the people at registration do know some of the other attendees, ask if they can introduce you to someone in your field.

2. Look for a Familiar Face. That's self-explanatory. The familiar face does not have to be a friend; they can be someone you've seen before or have been briefly introduced to or even someone you've heard about in the industry. When you are at a professional event, it's easy to talk about your professional goals. This is how you make connections!

- **Plan B**. Look for someone in the room who is NOT currently engaged in conversation. Chances are they are new to the event, just like you, and are dying for somebody to talk to from being the wallflower. This is your first new buddy. Help each other out here for Pete's sake; you're both in the same boat.

3. **Work the Room.** Pay attention to the room and the people around you. There will be a lot of people talking in small or large groups, but try to locate the *facilitators*…i.e. those people who are often seen *introducing* different people to other groups. Facilitators are experienced networkers and well-respected professionals whose recommendations carry weight. They are usually easy to talk to and happy to give guidance or provide short-term mentoring. This will make your night into a great success.

4. **Dig Deeper.** To optimize on time and build relationships, work on these essential guidelines with each person:

- Talk about yourself AND get to know the other person

- Share your own goals, but also be interested in other people's professional objectives

- Exchange contact information

- Discuss how you can help the new connection towards achieving their goals

- Conclude the conversation with an open to-do item, so that the networking can move forward

It's A Networker's World

At an offline-networking event, you can often times collaborate with other networkers to gain mutual traction towards your respective goals. Some of the ways to do that are:

1. **Trade in a Skill.** If you have a specific skill, offer discounted consulting to a small- or medium-sized business, in exchange for a strong introduction or recommendation to another client.

- "You've shown remarkable weight loss and fitness improvement in the last 12 weeks. I'd love to train the other members of your company, and if you guys do a corporate membership, I can give you 2 weeks free."

- "I'm glad you liked our digital prints for your biggest client. We do banner printing too and need help to connect with the right person there. If you can help us in this regard, I'd be happy to give you a 30% discount on your next order with us."

2. **Create Value for Others.** If you have a skill, offer to train people on the basics and enable them to introduce you to their key groups. For <u>ex</u>: If you're a tax professional, conduct a free 2-hour web seminar on lesser-known tax exemptions for small businesses. Collect testimonials and referrals from registered participants.

- "It's been a busy tax season and thank you for your business. This summer I will be hosting a 2-hour, complimentary session for our existing clients to help them identify tax saving opportunities during the year. Please feel free to bring your friends or coworkers along. There will be a meet-and-greet too for local businesses."

- "At the industry convention this year, I want to focus on educating small businesses about managing their social media. That's my area of expertise, and I would be happy to partner long-term with businesses that are serious about reaching their customers through social media."

3. **Be a Connection.** Help out others and network to see the possibilities for yourself.

<u>Example</u>: Introducing your kids' school director to your company's manufacturing head to arrange for a school field trip to the campus, as part of your organization's community participation. You may now have more interactions on neutral ground with the CXO, thus higher visibility in the company.

One of networking's key features is that not only do you connect to people but you can also <u>help others connect</u> for their benefit, too.

Remember what-goes-around-comes-around. Remember different strategies for different people and roles? Need more analogies...?

Remember that a network is group of systems, and in this case people, all interconnected with each other. This investment you make in other people's success will build goodwill for you and will come back to help you tenfold.

"You can make more friends in two months by becoming interested in other people than you can in two years by trying to get other people interested in you." - **Dale Carnegie**

CHAPTER 6

Follow-Up and Repeat

Maintenance

Irrespective of when you start networking and with what purpose, the very nature of networking requires you to stay engaged and moving. Once you've been through the first three steps, follow- up where needed and close the loop, where required.

If you have connected with someone, do not hesitate to follow-up. Generally, people follow-up to gently remind or request their connections to take a certain action…but you can also follow-up in other ways:

1. Write or call your contacts – personal visits will give you more time to discuss, learn and connect.

- Do not underestimate the power of old-world charm. You can go to any dollar store and get thank you cards. Sending someone a thank you card or a letter is an old-fashioned way of making a new-world impression. An old-fashioned business card can do the trick, too. Don't forget to include your phone number, website address, and social media links.

2. Stemming off of this, don't be afraid to invite someone out face-to-face for coffee or lunch.

3. Create a connection between two people in your network – same logic about you investing in other people's goals.

4. Invite your connection to an event (training, networking, etc.). This will give your connection an

opportunity to meet more people and also spend more time with you.

Let's not forget Jordan for the last time – she was very excited about all the connections she made at the offline event. Once she was back home, she took the time to carefully send out emails to each person thanking them for their time. She also personalized the message by using one of the above-mentioned follow-up anchors.

Polylogue

Polylogue is a discussion involving three or more people. This sort of conversation means that information *moves* in multiple directions.

In relevance to networking, that means there is more than one way to reach your networking goal. You have your list and your core message, now you need to understand how best you can capture the attention of your audience.

Talking in terms of an equation - people talk about things that capture their interest; so you need to *pay attention to other people's interests* in order to *have them be interested in what you want to do.*

Here are some basic guidelines for you to keep up with your networking efforts:

1.) Find a person to network with.

2.) Generate interest in what you can do for THEM first – share your goals/interests/skills and ask the other person questions about themselves, as well.

3.) Uncover common interests and goals.

4.) Find opportunities to collaborate.

5.) Create next steps towards mutual advantages.

6.) Follow-up.

7.) Stay in communication for improved relationships and growing results.

CHAPTER 7

Closing a Network

David And Goliath

From the local bakery to the President of the United States, almost everyone needs some amount of professional networking to take them further in achieving their goals.

Simply speaking, networking is meeting a stranger and building a connection between the two of you.

Gone are the days when a person would join an organization at 21 and retire from the same company 45 years later. Professionals today are ambitious and far-reaching. Meeting your goals in today's world is virtually impossible without networking.

Think of networking as an investment into your professional goals. A good investment will result in strong returns.

However, what networking is <u>not</u>: an overnight success mantra, for the unenthused, insincere or confused professionals. It is certainly *not* taking advantage of others and failing to reciprocate their generosity.

So start in your comfort zone, with the people you know. Reconnect and then take it forward to a bigger canvas.

A Networker's Checklist

Your networking checklist should include the following:

1. **Focusing on Your Why.** Don't lose sight of your objective. The clearer you are, the crisper your message

will be and the likelihood is higher that people will want to engage with you.

2. Have a Clear Self-Introduction. Write to or talk to people and share your purpose. The more questions people ask, the more you are able to present your ideas.

3. Ask for Advice. The only way to get one great idea is to first get plenty of good ideas. Ask people about their advice or opinions. This will engage their interest. Look for opportunities to collaborate, connect, grow or change.

4. Collaboration. Listen and show interest in other people's agendas. Find common objectives. This will lead to mutual gain.

5. Present Your Aspirations. There is no need for subtlety. Clearly present your professional aspirations and how the other person can impact your movement towards those goals. People are usually happy to help when they know they can make a difference.

6. **Share Stories, Experiences and Insights.** Networking is pretty laidback for the most part. There's no reason to be nervous. Share your experiences and really get to know people. Learn from their experiences, gain insights into their environment, make it an easy-flowing conversation and build a connection.

7. **Quality Over Quantity.** You don't have to network with everyone. Just like fishing, you won't ever catch every one out there. You just need to focus on building key contacts.

It is inadequate to say that networking is just about people....networking is about people *with ideas* and it is for *building opportunities*. Networking is about utilizing relationships and spreading ideas that enable learning and progress.

So don't let the whole concept of networking intimidate you…networks turn into relationships…and that's what business is all about!

Now You Know!

We have now gone from - *NOT knowing*...to *KNOWING*.

Doesn't it feel great? As cliché as the proverbial saying goes: knowledge is, indeed, power. The more you know, the more empowered you become. Not knowing is defeating, as you succumb to feelings of helplessness and surrendering of your own self.

Of course, acquiring knowledge is a never-ending quest. There is a great saying by Nobel Prize French author Andre Gide: "Believe those who are seeking the truth. Doubt those who find it."

At the very least, we hope we have set you off in the right path in regards to what you have set out to know, and that you have enjoyed our little journey together for the time you have spent with us.

If you can tell us how we did, that would be very appreciated! We value your feedback and always look forward to hearing from you, or if there is any way we could improve the entire experience for you. If you have a success story, even better - please let us know!

http://www.KnowItExpress.com

Don't forget to stay in contact for we would love to connect with you.

https://www.facebook.com/KnowItExpress
https://twitter.com/KnowItExpress
https://plus.google.com/+KnowItExpress

What would you like to know? Let us know!

CONTACT US

Now onward for more power to you, and thank you!